Let's Talk About
INTERRUPTING

Let's Talk About
INTERRUPTING

By JOY BERRY

Illustrated by John Costanza
Edited by Kate Dickey
Designed by Abigail Johnston

GROLIER ENTERPRISES CORP.

Let's talk about INTERRUPTING.

You are interrupting when you do something that makes it difficult for people to think.

You are interrupting when you do something that causes people to stop what they are doing.

You are interrupting when you talk when other people are talking.

When someone interrupts you:

- How do you feel?
- What do you think?
- What do you do?

When someone interrupts you,

- you may feel frustrated and angry,

- you may think, "I do not enjoy being around this person," or

- you may decide to stay away from the person.

It is important to treat other people the way you want to be treated.

If you do not want others to interrupt you, you must not interrupt them.

Try not to interrupt people who are thinking or trying to do something.

- Avoid talking to them.
- Do not make noises that would bother them.
- Do not do things that would distract them.

Try not to interrupt people who are talking to you.

- Allow them to finish talking before you speak.

- Say, "Excuse me," if you must interrupt them.

Try not to interrupt people who are talking to each other.

- Do not talk with them or listen to what they are saying unless they want you to do so.

- Do not get in between people who are talking to each other.

- Say, "Excuse me," if you must interrupt people who are talking.

Try not to interrupt people who are talking on the telephone.

- Avoid talking to them.

- Do not do anything that would make it difficult for them to hear.

- Do not do anything that would make it difficult for them to think about what they are doing.

Try not to interrupt people who are listening to something or watching TV.

- Avoid talking to them.

- Do not make noises that would make it difficult for them to listen.

- Do not change the channels on the TV unless they want you to do so.

- Do not get between them and the TV.

Try not to interrupt people who are watching a movie or a performance.

- If you must pass in front of others to get to your seat, do so quickly and quietly.

- Do not talk loudly or make other disturbing noises.

- Eat your food neatly and privately if eating is permitted.

- Do not hit or kick the seat in front of you or beside you.

- If possible, stay seated until the movie or performance is over.

Try not to interrupt people who are resting or sleeping.

- If possible, stay away from them.

- Be as quiet as you can so that you will not disturb them.

No one likes to be interrupted. If you do not want people to interrupt you, you should not interrupt them.